A WAAF AT WAR

.— .—— .— .— ..—

C
BALLOONS TO
BLETCHLEY PARK

BY MARGARET WILSON
(AS TOLD TO SIMON MAHONEY)

'You have to do your bit, don't you.'

DEDICATION

To Samuel and my family.

All proceeds from the sale of this book will go to charities that have given so much in time and resources, and are an invaluable part of my life.

IN GRATITUDE

We would like to thank the following organisations without whose help this book would still be just an idea.

In alphabetical order:

ARNO (Association of Royal Navy Officers)
Barrow-in-Furness Women's Co-operative
Blind Veterans UK
Royal British Legion

Our special thanks for His Majesty's Lord-Lieutenant of Derbyshire for agreeing to write the Foreword.

Authorship is an activity supported by an incredible number of other people. We are grateful for the support of those listed below and apologise if we have left anyone out inadvertently.

Our thanks go to:

Denise and Heather for contribution to the cover concept created by Simon Mahoney.

To Bev, Carrie, Heather, Mo and Sylvia for consumer testing the pre-edited manuscript.

To Denise for her tireless support, enthusiasm and research.

To Brian and Kay for prompting and supporting Margaret.

To Liz, Mary, Liz and William at Blind Veterans.

To Mike at ARNO.

To Becky at Barrowful.

To Adelle, Fiona and Brell at the Royal British Legion.

To all at More Than Words (https://www.morethan-words.com):

Alice Kennedy for the stunning cover, Clint MacDonald for typesetting for print, converting to E format and publishing, and to Kimberley for her usual editorial transformation of the manuscript.

A particular thanks to Kimberley who, in spite of an appalling motorcycle accident which almost destroyed her hands, insisted carrying on editing in the face of dreadful pain and severe practical difficulties.

To Mo Pickering-Symes for proof reading the final text.

CONTENTS

Foreword *by HM Lord-Lieutenant of Derbyshire* xi

Introduction *by Simon Mahoney*   15

Chapter One – To Childhood's End   19
Chapter Two – Joining in   35
Chapter Three – Becoming a Ballooneer   45
Chapter Four – The Barrow Girls   53
Chapter Five – Radios at Last   85
Chapter Six – Come into my Parlour ...   95
Chapter Seven – The Heart of the Web   103

Reflections   115
A Note from the Family   117
Additional Information   123
Morse Code   129
Glossary of Terms   131

FOREWORD

I am very honoured and grateful for the opportunity to endorse this delightful book, written by and featuring two remarkable and resourceful Derbyshire personalities.

The acclaimed author, Simon Mahoney, has had a varied career as a former Royal Marines young officer, social work team leader, and freelance artist. Simon, who completely lost his sight in 2018, writes with the help of a specially adapted PC and word-processing software provided by the charity Blind Veterans UK, which is where he met the redoubtable Margaret Wilson, whose story he was determined to tell.

Simon has given us a marvellous and endearing snapshot into Margaret's wartime experiences, an understated life of service and dedication to country and community. Despite it being nearly eighty years ago, the detail of Margaret's service in the WAAF (Women's Auxiliary Air Force) during World War II is incredible. It is a fresh and enlightening journey into a most significant time in our nation's history; a brilliant narrative told by Simon with humour, clarity, compassion and admiration.

The work at Bletchley made such an incredible contribution to the war effort it is estimated to have 'shortened the war by approximately two years' (Sir Harry Hinsley). But so little is known of these indominatable women and their physically demanding roles, their fears, the dangers, the secrecy, and the camaraderie that kept them going.

A WAAF at War is a feast of glorious detail into the world of war through a woman's eyes, brought to life through Margaret's tremendous memories and Simon's creative skills. We are able to reflect on their challenges and insights, and be thankful for so many who came before us in the hope of creating a better world, and give thanks, too, for those who today continue to give their time and talents to improve the lives of others.

One of the great pleasures of being His Majesty's Lord-Lieutenant for the county of Derbyshire is the opportunity to meet and celebrate some truly exceptional people. Simon and Margaret are certainly up there with the best.

I hope you all enjoy this book.

Elizabeth Fothergill CBE
HM Lord-Lieutenant of Derbyshire

INTRODUCTION

I first met Margaret about four years ago when I was telephone befriending for Blind Veterans. Margaret and myself range among the ranks of that organisation. As time went on – nearly four years – I began to appreciate what a truly fascinating and formidable woman Margaret was. She still is.

Margaret was born in 1923 as an Edwardian, matured as a Georgian, and lived her life as an Elizabethan. At what most would consider to be old age, she is still busy going into schools to talk to children about her life, sometimes with up to five groups in succession, leading numerous groups within Blind Veterans, and talking to any group who will ask her to attend. Additionally, regardless of the weather, she will always be found either at the Cenotaph or at a local war memorial every Armistice Day. To cap it all, sometime in the near future, she is to be distinguished by the award of the Légion d Honneur.

During the last world war, Margaret served in the WAAF – the Women's Auxiliary Air Force. It was a career which was a mixture of brutally physical and potentially dangerous endeavour, and highly skilled ultra-secret work. So secret that, even today, she will not talk about it in any detail. This accounts for the lack of any technical details concerning her career as a radio operator.

She was truly one of Churchill's geese that 'laid the golden eggs and never cackled'.

Having listened to her stories for some years, Margaret and I were talking one day and I said she should write a book. 'I am not like that,' she replied. 'I could not do that. I leave that sort of thing to you.' In that moment a mad idea was born.

This is Margaret's book, as told to me. Be quite sure that she is the author; I just typed it up. I have, however, added footnotes where I felt it was appropriate.

The book is a collection of Margaret's memories for her family and many friends and admirers. We hope others will also enjoy and be inspired by them.

It is an amazing story. All the more amazing in that it happened to an ordinary young woman from an ordinary town in an ordinary county. She, like so many others, simply went before she was called. You could say, an ordinary generation doing extraordinary things under desperate circumstances ... would this generation have done the same?

Simon Mahoney
Ashbourne, January 2023

CHAPTER ONE

TO CHILDHOOD'S END

---

*'Looking back, I realise we lived a
very idyllic and sheltered life ...'*

– Author

A story has to start somewhere. Mine started on 12 February 1923 when I was born in the post-World War I baby boom. My parents had both been actively involved in the Great War. My father had served as a sergeant in the Sherwood Foresters, and my mother was in the Land Army. We were not a large family by the standards of the time, there being only us three children, as I just had an older brother and much younger sister. Father was employed on the railway, and we lived in a council house in Shirebrook, Derbyshire, with a big garden.

About the time I was born, both of my parents became very involved in the Parish Council. They were civic minded, and no doubt regarded as pillars of the local community. I must have been influenced by this, as I started selling poppies at the age of twelve, and have done so ever since.

Probably my earliest memories stem from the time that my parents were asked by the local council to provide accommodation in our house for the district nurses, when I was about three years old. This must have been regarded as rather fortunate as they now had resident babysitters. This was obviously something of a godsend, as it enabled them to go to the many council meetings. The nurses taught me the basics, how to put a sling on someone and so on. From this early age I was encouraged to watch them working, and learned a huge amount of first aid from them, which has been useful all my life.

In the end the nurses stayed with my parents for eighteen years, and were eventually moved into a house across the road only towards the end of the war. Even when I came back home in 1946 I used to drop in and give them a hand.

We were lucky to live in Shirebrook, a quiet little coal mining town. This was in the district of Bolsover on the border of Derbyshire and Nottinghamshire. Despite the fact that we lived in tumultuous times, such as the Great Depression and the General Strike, as children we were totally unaware of it. Looking back I realise we lived an idyllic, innocent and very sheltered life. We had a radio by the time I was six, but we rarely listened to it. With a large garden, and the kids' play area on the recreation ground just down the road, we were too busy 'playing out'. Then it was meal time, and then to bed.

Like so many other people, I left school at the age of fourteen. I started a job in a little sweetshop on Station Road on the day of my fourteenth birthday. This was before rationing, and we sold all sorts of sweets from toffees and humbugs to 'modern' boiled sweets like Rhubarb and Custard and Pear Drops. The owner of the sweetshop was also clerk to the council. He was not a very healthy man, and when he was poorly I used to help him with his council work.

After a year or so I started to work at the local Co-op. I was still there when the war broke out. I have to admit I was oblivious to what was going on outside our little town, as my parents were so careful to shield us from the real world. I had absolutely no awareness we were sliding into a war that no one wanted.

When Poland was finally invaded by Germany and it was declared that war had started, my father gathered us children together to tell us. He told us that we were at war, and he hoped that it would not be like the last time when he had to go away to fight. He also said to us that we should try not to worry, not to think about it, that it would be over soon, and it was best to just 'trust the upper ones' who would soon get rid of it. Four months later rationing was introduced [Note 1], and it was still running sixteen months later when I became old enough to join in.

At the outbreak of war I was sixteen and a half years old. Apart from having to take gas masks everywhere with us, life continued much as before. One bit of excitement was when a bomb was dropped on the edge of town. Fortunately nobody was hurt and no major damage was caused. We were in bed at the time and the ceiling came down and, as far as I can remember, we were fine, shook the plaster off the bed and got back in. Unlike many other people we did not have our own shelter.

Leaving aside the need to carry gas masks and occasional shortages at this time, the only reminder of the war was the German prisoners of war. We would see them, not very often admittedly, doing a bit of gardening or wall building. Apart from that they did not appear in our lives at all.

With my parents being very aware of their duty to serve the public, it was inevitable that I would immediately join the Civil Defence and the Women's Royal Voluntary Service (WRVS). This I did both with my mother and with her encouragement. (I continued with the WRVS and poppy selling for the British Legion when I came back from the WAAF.)

The town being very quiet, and relatively isolated, the war did not really touch us. Involvement with the Civil Defence and WRVS was mainly meetings about what was happening on the various fronts, who had been bombed locally, training for meeting emergencies and so on. In spite of the intense practice and extensive preparations, we never had to deal with any real situations, certainly none that involved risk to property, life or limb. At this point, and even later, it was hard to take the war seriously. From the briefings we knew about what had been going on, but even when the fight moved nearer home with the air battles over Kent and the Blitz, it was hard to relate it to our lives.

One thing that impacted on all of us was the rationing. This was introduced in the February of 1940, more or less on my seventeenth birthday! We were lucky in that Mum was a good cook. This meant she was adept at making the best of what was available. As mentioned previously, we very luckily had a large garden, and this provided us with a lot of vegetables and we never really went short. If we needed something a little bit special … well, let's just say I worked at the Co-op. Say no more!

One regular activity was the fire watching. This was carried out at my workplace, the local Co-op, and was great fun. We did this duty in shifts, four of us girls and an undermanager. They brought bunkbeds down for us, into the shoe department, where we were posted for the fire watching, and a table and chairs.

The great thing was that they fed us, with the undermanager doing the cooking. To be honest, the meals were much better than we could get at home, even with my mum's cooking skills, as they took the food from the stock in the shop. It was here that I was first introduced to the joys of baked beans on toast!

If the air raid sirens sounded, the fire brigade would come down and station themselves outside the shop. Every now and again they would come in and do some operational training with us girls. This was mainly showing us the fire points and what to do if a fire broke out. Whilst we knew this well enough, it made for a more enjoyable shift!

The fire-watching shifts were uneventful most of the time. On many occasions we occupied ourselves reckoning up from the day's trading. This of course was done in our heads, as there were no machines or calculators in those days. We did not think it was strange, because that was the way we were taught.

It was sometimes quite eerie in there when we were doing our shift. Because of the blackout regulations we were allowed only dim lighting. In addition to that, all the windows were very heavily blacked out. The threat was considered to be very real, and nobody could show a light in case it helped the bombers to find us.

My brother had already left home to join the army. As a consequence, after my seventeenth birthday, I started to consider my own future. I began to really think seriously about what I wanted to do when I was old enough to join the war.

I decided I would like to be an RAF (Royal Air Force) radio operator. I have no idea why I was so set on it. It just appealed to me. Looking back, I realise I had not the faintest clue about what radio operators did or what was involved, but I am so glad I was absolutely determined this was going to happen – and I was not disappointed, because I ended up loving every minute of it.

My mother, for some reason, was not at all happy at the thought of me going into the forces. She kept saying that she thought I was far too frail and little to do it. She was quite convinced I would not be able to cope with the physical side. Thinking about it now, I feel she may not have understood why I wanted to join up when I was not liable for conscription until I was twenty, a good two years in the future. Not unnaturally she was rather resistant to that whole idea too, and did her best to try to encourage me to go into nursing. In spite of my experiences with the district nurses, I just could not see this as the way I wanted to make my contribution to the war effort.

Whilst my mother's misgivings and opposition were one problem, there was, unfortunately, another. If I had wanted to be an RAF telephonist or office worker there would have been no difficulty, but the particular specialism I had had set my heart on, because of its nature, needed the written consent of both parents for anyone under the age of twenty – at least that is what I was led to understand. It seemed I was to be thwarted, after all. Mother, being totally opposed to this, was absolutely steadfast in her refusal to sign the necessary papers. Fortunately, my father was all for it, and somehow the problem was resolved: both signatures were mysteriously appended to my documents. To this day I have no idea who he managed to persuade to sign the papers as my mother. As far as I know, nobody has ever owned up to it! I think it's possible it may have been one of my aunties, which my dad and I kept from my mother for as long as possible. In the end she had to be told, however, and, to be fair, did accept it.

I had to go up to Nottingham for a few pre-enlistment tests and a medical examination, and mother used to accompany me. I never risked asking if she realised I was still joining with the intention of becoming a radio operator. Sometimes you have to let sleeping dogs lie.

In the January of 1941, one month before my eighteenth birthday, I joined the Women's Auxiliary Air Force (WAAF), and exchanged the Co-op for the great adventure of leaving home and joining up. This was truly childhood's end and they gave me a little prayer book when I left, from the Gospel of John. It is something I still have and treasure to this day.

Being nearly eighteen, I had a boyfriend. His name was Samuel, and he was nearly twenty and working at one of the local factories. Later he was conscripted into the pit and he became a Bevin Boy [Note 2].

Samuel was not very happy about my going away, particularly as it was from choice. He did, however, recognise this was something I wanted to do and was supportive. He accepted it as he knew that once I had made my mind up there was no chance of changing it.

Over the next five tumultuous years the one constant was that we wrote to each other three times a week, come what may. Somehow we managed that distance relationship, as did millions of others, and when all the nonsense was finally over I was, at long last, able to marry my Bevin Boy.

NOTES FOR CHAPTER ONE

Note 1

Rationing

The British Government introduced food rationing at the beginning of 1940. This was to make sure that everybody, regardless of income, had a fair share in a time of national shortages. Every man, woman and child was given a ration book with coupons. These were needed to buy rationed goods.

Basics like sugar, meat, fats, bacon and cheese were directly rationed, and you had to register with particular shops like the butcher, greengrocer or baker separately.

The ration itself was calculated at the minimum an adult required to keep healthy, if still hungry. Obesity was not a problem in those days!

One unintended consequence of this was the growth of a thriving black market. To some extent it still exists.

The weekly ration for an adult was as follows:

1 fresh egg
2 ounces of butter [56 grams]
4 ounces of margarine [113 grams]
2 ounces of loose tea [56 grams]
1 ounce of cheese [28 grams]
8 ounces of sugar [226 grams]
4 ounces or 4 thin rashers of bacon [113 grams]
3 pints of milk [1.7 litres]
1s 2d (1 shilling and two pence worth) of meat per
    week
1 pound of jam per fortnight [450 grams]

Rations did however fluctuate throughout the 1940s. Tinned goods, dried fruit, cereals and biscuits were rationed using a points system, with the number of points allocated changing according to availability.

Priority allowances of milk and eggs were given to those most in need, including children and expectant mothers.

As shortages increased, long queues were taken for granted. It was not unusual for someone to reach the front of a long queue, only to find out that the item they had been waiting for had just run out.

Not all foods were rationed. Fruit and vegetables were never rationed, but were often in short supply, and this led directly to the 'dig for victory' movement, where all available land was used for planting and growing.

Both clothing and petrol were also included in the rationing scheme.

Rationing continued into the early fifties, only ending in 1954 when meat at last became freely available.

Note 2

The Bevin Boys

Whilst we were fighting for our life on the various battle fronts, this did not diminish the need for coal for the war effort at home. Initially, many young miners were conscripted for the armed forces, but by 1942 it became clear we were not producing enough coal because we were short of miners. An appeal for volunteers and various incentive schemes failed to fill the gap, so in 1943, Ernest Bevin, Minister for Labour and National

Service in the coalition government, introduced conscription to the coal mines.

From that time, one in ten of conscripts went to the mines ... and became known as Bevin Boys. In spite of doing dangerous and nasty work, they were regarded as cowards and 'draft dodgers' by some. In addition to that, their contribution to the war effort was not recognised until 1995.

CHAPTER TWO

JOINING IN

---

*'The indignation over a bit of fluff had
to be witnessed to be believed …'*

– Author

Finally, after the slightly rocky ride at home, the
medicals and tests, I set out to actually join up. I
caught the early six o'clock train to Nottingham
and my dad cycled across Shirebrook to see me
off. I was lucky to meet up with my best friend,
who just happened to be catching the same train.
It was a lovely surprise! She was going off to join
the Land Army and we were both excited at what

the future held. She and I were not to meet again until after the war in 1946.

At Nottingham I was met by a man in civilian dress covered in badges, and he took me to where other recruits from our region were assembled. He then left me, and I never saw him again. There were only five of us and we took the seven o'clock train to Bridgnorth in the county of Shropshire as instructed by our joining orders.

The train was crowded with many other young people going off to join up, but the five of us chatted all the way, never bothering to even look out of the window.

The journey was probably less than eighty miles as the crow flies but, being short of crows, the steam train did not arrive until mid-afternoon. I can't be sure, but I think it must have taken seven or eight hours. I know we were very grateful for a cup of tea when we eventually arrived.

When we finally left the train at Bridgnorth station, we met up with eight other recruits, and were quickly located and corralled by a tough-looking WAAF officer who bundled us into a large car, or perhaps it was a minibus. I had never been in any sort of car before, and that was when the fun began.

To my eyes, Bridgnorth was quite strange. It seemed to me to have been built on two levels, with the shops all up the top and the houses down below, divided by the River Severn through the middle. Little did we realise, as we passed through it, that the strange little town was something we would not have a chance to explore. Once we entered RAF Bridgnorth [Note 1], and No. 1 Recruit Training Depot, that was it. We would have no chance to leave it to look at the town.

When our intake squad was finally formed there were twenty of us, all very young, from various backgrounds, all shapes and sizes, and apprehensively eyeing each other up and the situation. Of course, once we were launched into our basic training regime there was very little time for anything, least of all eyeing each other up.

Like everybody else who has gone through basic training, we were subjected to a routine that barely allowed time to think. Collecting our kit, the issuing of our uniforms, and learning how to look after and wear them took a couple of days; adapting to the wholly different and almost alien world of the RAF took a great deal longer.

There was the nonsense of stripping our beds every morning and making a bed pack with our bedding. They had to be precisely made and immaculate. Each morning before breakfast we had to scrub out our accommodation and arrange our lockers strictly according to regulations. Perfection was the only acceptable standard.

Our accommodation, lockers, bed packs and persons were closely inspected by eagle-eyed officers and sergeants, and it was always an occasion for suspense and high drama. The heights of horror and indignation expressed by our betters over a bit of fluff had to be witnessed to be believed. Very impressive indeed! God forgive you if anything was wrong, manky or out of place, because our officers would not!

Our days were filled with lectures about the RAF, the regulations that applied to us, the various options we might be offered, and how and who to salute. This of course was against a background of relentless physical training – and the inevitable 'square-bashing' – marching to a military drill – designed to turn us from a rabble into highly disciplined, quick-thinking aircraftwomen. Every movement around the base was in concert. We marched and did everything as a squad in all our waking moments, and there was no escape from the constant harrying and chivvying from our corporals and sergeant.

The remorseless activity and harrying–cheerfully referred to as 'beasting' – was all designed to turn us from civilians to aircraftwomen in the shortest possible time. It also began to transform us into a close-knit group. We very quickly learned the value of comradeship and mutual support under pressure, one of the great strengths of the armed forces. On top of this of course was the development of the ghastly 'gallows humour' which characterises most people who have been in the forces, and did not exclude us girls!

There were times when we were sharply reminded we were no longer the complete owners of ourselves. One of the things that impressed upon us that the RAF owned us body and soul was the various inoculations. There was no such thing as consent or refusal. I took badly to mine and ended up in bed for a day. I think that was about the only time I had to myself during the whole of basic.

The whole process was intended to transform us from a gaggle of girls and make us part of the Air Force as quickly as possible. We had to emerge as disciplined airwomen who would obey orders without arguing, and yet still have a degree of mental alertness. I guess it must have worked, as within a few weeks I was doing some crazy things that nobody in their right mind would ordinarily consider, let alone do.

We had only been there for a couple of weeks when we were asked to say what branch of the service we fancied. We were given a list of about twenty options. The only thing that appealed to me was the barrage balloons. But this was not an informed choice; rather, it was the not knowing what it was that made it seem better than the others, which were rather domestic and, to my mind, not really contributing to the war. Though I had no idea what a barrage balloon was, I felt this might be an interesting fill in until I could get on a radio operators course.

The barrage balloon training course was starting in a week or so. Consequently, I only spent three weeks on basic training before it was time to leave for the course at RAF Wythall in Birmingham. To my great joy I discovered that nearly all of us, eighteen out of the twenty, had chosen the same option!

Just before we left we had the passing out parade from basic. To our great pleasure it was the king himself, King George VI, who took the salute. With that wonderful boost to our morale, we went off to our war.

NOTES FOR CHAPTER TWO

Note 1

RAF Bridgnorth

RAF Bridgnorth was a Royal Air Force station, created after the outbreak of World War II on 6 November 1939 at Stanmore, and situated to the east of the town. As RAF Stanmore Park already existed in Middlesex, it was named RAF Bridgnorth. Although during its existence various static aeroplanes were displayed as Gate Guardians, RAF Bridgnorth never had a runway. Appropriately, the unit badge bore the Latin motto 'Haec porta moenia viri'; or 'This is the gate, our men are the walls'.

The first unit stationed there was No. 4 Recruit Centre. Their role was to carry out the basic training of new recruits in the RAF, originally designed for 2,000 recruits and 500 permanent staff.

In 1940, spare accommodation at Bridgnorth enabled it to be used as a transit and kitting-out centre for troops returning from Dunkirk.

Towards the end of the year it was able to resume its primary role of training WAAF recruits, including Margaret, and it changed name to No.1 WAAF Depot in January 1941.

CHAPTER THREE

BECOMING A BALLOONEER

---

*'We made a game of counting the shrapnel
as it hit the roof. Tic-tic-tic ...'*

– Author

We had become a coherent squad through basic and it was a bonus that we were, nearly all of us, to pass together onto the next phase of our life in the WAAF. We arrived at RAF Wythall, the headquarters of No. 6 Barrage Balloon Centre. They were tasked with providing the barrage balloon defence for Coventry, Birmingham and the surrounding district. They also had the additional role of training new recruits.

We were all looking forward to learning about our new specialism but, as you can imagine, Bridgnorth and our new billet were worlds apart. For one thing, we were no longer raw recruits on basic training, we were on an operational training course and our treatment was very different. No more square-bashing, physical training, bed packs or bullshine (totally unnecessary activities!). It was wonderful!

We were still members of the armed forces, however, and we could not avoid marching altogether. We were marched as a class from our quarters to the classroom, and from the classroom to where we did our practical training. It was part of being a WAAF we could not entirely avoid.

A major change was that we were bombed most nights at Birmingham. Every evening the sirens started up, and just the sound could make our blood run cold. Sometimes, when the raids were early, we could get to the air raid shelter, where we stopped all night; but if the bombers came later in the evening we had to shelter under our beds. We must have looked very strange indeed. Regulations required that we wore our great coats and tin lid, and had our gas masks slung around our necks. And there we would lay, with all this gear on over our night clothes, and our slippers on our feet.

The beds were so low to the ground that we ended up lifting them up onto our shoulders. We had to stay there like that until morning. We could hear the shrapnel from the anti-aircraft guns pattering onto the roof. We used to make a game of counting it as separate pieces slid down the roof – tic-tic-tic – and hit the ground. We could sometimes hear the aircraft, the banging of the guns and the whistle of bombs.

In the morning, when we finally crawled out from under our beds, we would go outside and all the shrapnel would be spread all over the ground. For some reason it never occurred to us to be frightened; we just took it all in our stride.

Whilst this was all going on there was also the small matter of the barrage balloon training course. Somehow in the midst of all this mayhem, little or no sleep, and overcrowding and craziness, we managed the demanding theoretical and practical aspects of the course. In less than three months we had to learn everything there was to know about balloons. At the end of this, we were expected to be able to manage all aspects of barrage balloon handling, in any weather, and both during daylight and night time.

Remarkably, most of us were able to finish and had learnt all we were supposed to about our new and highly specialised duties. At the end of the course we had to sit the tests. I have to admit that I romped them. Sadly, some of the girls failed, and so we lost some of our original group.

It was not until much later we learned that we were an experimental group. They wanted to see if they could use WAAFs for the balloons to allow men to be released for other duties. Also, we were the first all-female group to be trained at the centre in Birmingham. We had arrived not knowing anything about the balloons or, indeed, what we were letting ourselves in for. It turned out to be physically demanding, challenging and full of potentially lethal hazards. Our training had been very thorough, however, and we felt confident we could perform well despite being unsupervised.

Because we were a female group of trainees we seemed to attract a great deal of attention.

This was not just within Balloon Command and the wider RAF, but also in the wider world. Towards the end of our training, when we had progressed to the point of launching a balloon with a modicum of dignity, we were visited by a film crew. We knew nothing about it and we were too busy to notice at the time. Looking at that film now, it's impossible to know whether to laugh or cry. It is very much of its time!

British Pathé News were the people who made that very short film about our group when we were still training. It is of course accompanied by suitably patriotic music, and the most enormous condescension. What they said on the film is worth relating:

'WAAFs are now being recruited to handle the balloon barrage to help release more men in the RAF for other operational duties. The balloon section of the WAAF are enlisting those sturdy types whom we habitually looked upon as cut out solely for gym mistresses, policewomen or mothers-in-law. These girls can fill a gas bag with the best of them. When it comes to pulling a few wires to get on in their job, Sgt Jerry is there to remind them a woman's work is never done. Well now the girls are going to send the balloon up.

The way they are handling all that tackle makes me think it won't be long now. Controlling the ascent is the bird in the golden cage. And there she goes! As pretty a launching as you would see anywhere. What's that saying about the hand that rocks the cable?'

Listen to it now and you want to cringe, but that was the way they talked about women in those days.

I, with seven other girls, were then sent off to our first operational posting in Balloon Command [Note 1]. This was a little daunting. No longer would we have the comfort of experienced instructors around us. This was going to be for real and, whilst a little apprehensive, we were all ready for it and wanting to get stuck in.

NOTES FOR CHAPTER THREE

Note 1

Balloon Command

Balloon Command was formed in 1938 as part of the rapid preparations for the war everybody knew was coming. It was an intrinsic part of the strategy to protect the civilian and military infrastructure from bombing. The other parts of this strategy were Fighter Command, the newly developed chain of radar stations, the Royal Observer Corps, the anti-aircraft guns and searchlights. Barrage balloons were also deployed at sea to protect convoys and the landings in Sicily and Normandy.

The balloons were typically worked by a crew of eight men and a senior NCO such as a sergeant. In early 1941 they decided to experiment with using women crews in a bid to release men for other duties. Margaret was in one of the first of these groups.

The job was physically demanding and had the potential to be hideously dangerous. The men and women who manned these balloons were definitely unsung heroes.

The main role of the balloons was to force the enemy to fly higher. Unfortunately, they also indicated the presence of a worthwhile target, so if an enemy bomber was being harried by a fighter they would often head for a barrage balloon and dump their bombs if they could not attain their primary target.

During the war the barrage balloons brought down 22 enemy aircraft out of 54 collisions. They also brought down over 300 friendly aircraft out of more than 900 collisions. As friendly aircraft traffic was very heavy over Britain in comparison to the enemy, this is not quite as bad as it seems.

Balloon Command was finally disbanded in October 1945.

CHAPTER FOUR

THE BARROW GIRLS

---

*'A mile of cable dropping on our heads was something
we did not want to think about!'*

– Author

We all took the train to Barrow-in-Furness. As
a group we had been together for nearly four
months. In that time we had all changed, but the
one thing we all had in common was excitement
at what the future held. Unlike the trip from
Nottingham to Bridgnorth, mercifully it only took
a couple of hours. The town was a place I had
never heard of and had not the remotest idea

where it was. Again we were met at the station by a WAAF officer who bundled the eight of us into a large car.

We finally arrived at the wireworks on the edge of town at Walney Road. Our particular balloon was positioned in the wireworks' yard, a massive great big field just across the road from the factory itself. I believe it is now a public park.

At first sight, our new home consisted of four Nissen huts huddled together, as if to ward off their loneliness. The sleeping quarters were set up in a couple of quite small huts, and there was a separate dining hut and ablution block. We had absolutely no idea how long we would have to stay there.

Although there were supposed to be three or four of us in each hut, we decided against it, and as a group we agreed to use just the one for all of us. This would be much warmer in winter and a lot more fun. As we rarely saw the WAAF officer, and didn't see our sergeant again, this went unchallenged. In fact we were basically left to ourselves, as our officer was concerned with a number of groups of WAAFs. We were provided with bunk beds, and I managed to get a bottom one as I was frightened of falling off the top.

After we had dumped our kit in the accommodation hut, which was very basic, we went to the dining room hut, which had a rough kitchen area. Unlike all the other local balloon crews we did not have our meals provided, we had to cook them ourselves. Two of us girls had to be on duty there, and we had to cook a meal for us all. As none of us could cook, somehow we muddled through, and if we needed to know anything we wrote home!

Each week our food was delivered to the site, and basic was again the word. We seemed to have tins of stew more than anything else. I hated the damned stuff with a vengeance, and still do to this day, but I quickly learnt that when you are hungry you will eat anything.

It was so much nicer when Betty French – she was a girl from Leicester –and I would go to the home of Captain and Mrs Robinson after church on a Sunday. They not only fed us potato cakes, they also let us both have a bath. There was only five inches (12.5 centimetres) of hot water, but after nothing but strip washes it was heaven. The curate from the church used to join us on these

Sundays, although not in the bath! That bath, potato cake, a slice of bread and butter with a cup of tea ... well, it was lovely, and went on for nearly a year, until I left.

Whilst the accommodation and dining room were lacking somewhat in simple comfort, the ablution block was in a class all of its own. The facilities in the washroom were more than a little crude. There was a long narrow concrete sink without a plug, and this delightful bit of kit was served by four cold water taps. Just to add to the fun, if we left water in a bowl or bucket overnight in winter we had to break the ice to wash! We were told that if we wanted hot water we could light a fire and heat it up in a tin, but as we had no tins this was simply not an option.

Luckily, after a couple of weeks the men from the wireworks learnt about what we had to put up with and they would very kindly bring us hot water in large containers. After we had washed in it, we would use the same water for our clothes. If the water situation wasn't bad enough, worse were the toilets. They were a real shock.

There were eight cubicles in the block with half doors, which was horror enough. But inside the cubicle was the real horror: large metal bins with a board across the top with a hole cut into it! I suppose we were lucky, though, as we heard that the men in the balloon unit before us had made the wooden seats for the metal bins.

Whoever was on the night watch had to deal with the toilets before the end of the shift, which was at 0600hrs. It was really not very nice. Every night a pair of us had to go to the top of this enormous field with each bin, dig a deep hole, tip the contents in and cover it up. The hole had to be in a different place each time, and in this way we worked our way around the top edge of the field. We took over the site at the beginning of May, and in the back of all our minds was what it was going to be like in winter when the ground was frozen. It was always a different pair of girls doing this. I was very little, and if I was paired with a tall girl, like my friend Betty French, the contents sometimes slopped over me. We laughed about it, but we could have cried.

It was at times like that the constant stream of letters from Samuel was such a comfort. Indeed, I often think that our letters kept us both grounded and, in a funny way, happy. Anyway, back to the reality of the bins!

We also had to scrub those wretched bins out, disinfect them and make sure they were dry. On returning to the wash house, we then had to scrub the boards on which they stood. Remember there were eight of these horrible things. After a couple of weeks we all agreed to only use six, and shortly after reduced it to four. We did try using two, but it made the bins far too heavy to carry. This sort of thing was not what I was used to. Still, we soon adapted and, in the end, we just took it as a normal part of the routine.

A few months after we established ourselves, the night watchman on the nearby slag heap noticed what we were doing. One night he called to us, telling us to stop and that he would do it for us. His kindness relieved us all of a horrible chore, and he was so much better at digging holes!

Without our really noticing it, the first six months passed. We had a good relationship with the nearby wireworks, and they did everything they could think of to make life a bit easier for us.

Our first Christmas loomed, and we were allowed to have a small party of twenty people or so. We had no decorations or anything, and one of the men brought us a rose bush from his garden to act as a Christmas tree. Other men saved the silver paper from cigarette packets as, working with a hydrogen-filled balloon, none of us smoked. With this and other scrounged bits and pieces we made decorations, dressed the 'tree', and invited our guests. Amongst them was Mr Black, who was manager of the wireworks, and his wife.

He was very nice, and showed a lot of interest in what we were doing and how we did it. He was very charming about our decorations and the effort we had made. We showed him around, and he was not too impressed with our ablution block! When he saw our wash house, and in particular the toilets, he was absolutely horrified. Without any hesitation he immediately insisted that we use the ladies' facilities in the factory. Bliss! White porcelain, hot running water and flushing toilets. What heaven! I have to admit, though, that in mid-winter at night it was too much of a fag to climb over the factory wall, so we used our own facilities.

The people at the factory were very kind to us. One day they made a wooden bench and put it in the factory entrance for us. In this way we could be relatively warm when doing the night watch.

It was little kindnesses like this that made life so much more bearable.

It was just as well they looked after us. No one else was. We discovered in pretty short order that, compared with the men, we were getting the thick end of the stick.

We also found out that we were the only balloon unit based on a field. But not only this, we were the only female unit – eight young girls with the most primitive conditions, whilst all the men had hot running water and proper toilets. Not forgetting, of course, they also had their meals provided! Perhaps the final insult was that the men were on two shillings a day (10p) and we were on one and fourpence (6.7p)!

So there we were. Eight teenagers, none of us very big, manning this big beast of a barrage balloon with no sergeant, and all living cheek to cheek and having to get on and work with each other. This in spite of the fact that we all came from varying back grounds and different parts of the country. This of course is the real value of basic training: we had all, through a shared process of beasting, hard work and indignity, been moulded into the RAF pattern.

The balloon itself was a great big brute of a thing, about sixty feet (18.3 metres) long and roughly twenty-four feet (7.3 metres) round. It was basically a bag filled with gas tethered to a cable which went to a hand-operated winch, which was within a cage to protect the operator if a cable should break.

There were eight big concrete blocks, to which it was also attached by cables. These not only prevented it from flying away, but also helped it to face into the wind when it was deployed as part of the balloon barrage. When the wind changed, we girls had to move the concrete blocks so the balloon kept into the wind and the cables did not become tangled.

Apart from the cables becoming tangled, if the balloon came off the wind it could swing wildly about and damage itself. Sometimes we had to move the blocks a long way; other times it was only a short distance. The blocks were big, far too heavy to lift, and we had to drag them. As said, most of us were only little but somehow we managed. There were times when I thought of my mum and what she would have said if she could have seen me doing this!

The launching and retrieval of the balloon was always a bit of a tense time. We had to ensure the cables from the winch were let out or brought in at the same rate. If we failed to do this, the balloon could go out of control with possibly lethal consequences for us all. This was particularly so if there was anything of a wind.

In addition to the juggling act with the cables, and the fact that the balloon was filled with highly flammable hydrogen, it had two features which made it even more tricky.

The first were wings or fins, which had to be unfolded when going up and folded in when it was on the ground. They were half up the side of the balloon and someone had to go up a long ladder to do it.

The other feature was a bomb, which was attached to the underside of the balloon. Apparently, the idea was that if enemy aircraft came near the balloon, the bomb could be detonated and destroy the aircraft. The bomb was triggered by hitting one of the nine cables. The fact that the explosion would possibly kill the balloon-handling crew was considered a risk worth taking.

Clearly, if the balloon was on the ground it would be very dangerous to have a live bomb just sitting there, so whilst on the ground the detonating mechanism was locked by a split pin. When the balloon was raised and it was well clear of the ground, someone had to go up the ladder to remove the pin and arm the bomb. On its return, the balloon had to be held off the ground and the split pin replaced to make the bomb safe.

Being the smallest in the unit, I was allocated both jobs. This was not quite what it might seem, as being the smallest made it easier for the other girls to hold the ladder steady. However, as someone who was afraid of falling off a top bunk, going up a long ladder was my particular nightmare. There was of course no question of refusing. You had to get on and do it.

We practised raising and lowering the balloon every morning and afternoon and, after a while, the ladder became routine and slightly less fearsome. We drilled hard with that brute of a balloon as we had to deploy and manoeuvre it in any weather, and by night as well as by day. After a while we became very fast with it, and we could match any male crew.

The balloon could operate up to 5,000 feet (1,520 metres), and one essential task was the frequent checking of the cables and their attachment to the balloon. Having one coming loose and nearly a mile of cable dropping on our heads was something we did not want to think about [Note 1]! As for the live bomb, well we just took it as part of the furniture and ignored the risk. What else were we supposed to do?

On one occasion the balloon got away from us. Although neither the bomb or the gas exploded, it was quite badly damaged. It took over a week to repair it.

When a balloon was damaged both the outside and the inside needed to be mended. It was our job to go into the inside of the balloon, when it was on the ground, obviously, and repair it. The smell was awful, almost enough to make you ill. I don't know if that was the gas or the material of which the balloon was made, but it was dreadful. Looking back, I think that was probably the most unpleasant but least dangerous part of the job with the balloons. Like everything else, we just took it in our stride.

There was one small mercy in this apparently endless list of hazards: the hydrogen for the balloon was not stored on site. If the balloon needed inflating, such as after repair, the hydrogen was brought to us from a central storage site.

When we were not drilling with, or deploying it, the balloon would be securely snugged on the ground, lashed to the concrete blocks to keep it tethered. When the alert was sounded, we had to go round all the lashings. The last ones to be done were those holding down what we called 'the wings'.

I have no idea whether any planes ever hit a barrage balloon. All I know is that ours always came back down. Considering the bomb in the base, that was always a relief.

It was hard work and also a lot of fun. It was also a very physical job, and I don't think too many people would want to do it today. The feeling we were doing something towards the war made it all worthwhile, though, and as a group we all became even closer.

We all worked that first Christmas, but throughout that nine-month period we managed to get away from the site for some home leave. A whole week at home was quite surreal. It was so far removed from what, for us, had become normal, and I think most of us were glad to get back to the reality of the other girls and the balloon. Whilst it was wonderful to see Samuel, too, it went in a flash. It didn't feel real. In many ways the balloon had taken over our lives and anything else, however pleasant, was an unwelcome distraction.

It was not all hard work. Occasionally we were allowed, in small numbers, to go into the local town. One day I came back from the town to find the site buzzing with amusement.

Apparently they'd had a streaker dash across the field, and I had missed it! I need not have worried. The next day he came back again, running around in all his glory (?)! We were then treated by the sight of the civvy cops chasing him in one direction, with the RAF Police (or 'snowdrops') converging on him from another. He was finally caught and bundled into a van. They wouldn't even let him put his trousers on!

On another occasion we had a Peeping Tom. We were quite friendly with a couple of 'red caps', or military police, and they offered to deal with him. One night they set off round the nearby bushes in opposite directions to see if they could catch him. As you might imagine, they ended up catching each other, much to our merriment!

Shortly after Christmas, nine months after arriving, and just as we were getting used to hot and cold running water and flushing loos, we were quietly moved from the wireworks and deployed in the dock area as more bombing was expected. The bonus was that we would continue to have hot and cold water, proper toilets and, at last, prepared meals. This almost made up for the added risk of being bombed.

I recall there was a raid on the docks [Note 2], but the bombers missed their target. As was so often the case, sadly the civilians were the main casualties. The docks themselves never lost a day of work.

We had arrived at the wireworks as a bunch of raw trainees. By the time we moved to the docks we had been moulded into a very well-knit team. Both physically and mentally every one of us had changed out of all recognition. We had blossomed. We had grown up.

We proved to be a good crew, even though our work with the balloon was, unbelievably, unsupervised. It was through hard work and huge amounts of common sense that we became very good at what we did. We started out as an experiment. They'd had no idea whether we could do the job. I think we showed them.

A few weeks after our move to the docks, my wireless operators course came through. It was with mixed feelings that I said goodbye to the brute and the girls to set off on the next step in my war.

NOTES FOR CHAPTER FOUR

Note 1

Accidents and Fatalities

Incredibly, only twelve people were killed and nine injured throughout the war in Balloon Command. Bearing in mind the fate of R101 and the Hindenburg, this is an extraordinary accolade for the quality of the training of the crews.

Note 2

Barrow Docks

The docks not only acted as an overspill port to receive cargoes from the Atlantic convoys, it was also an important shipbuilding centre. They built both merchant ships and warships, the latter ranging from aircraft carriers, cruisers, destroyers, and frigates to submarines, including the famous *HMS Illustrious, HMS Ajax, HMS Upholder*, and *HMS Jervis Bay.* They were producing warships throughout the war and continue to this day.

Margaret

Margaret training for wireless operator

Training for wireless operator with Mrs Robinson.
Margaret, third from left, top row, 1943

A Watch on the stepladders used for unfurling the barrage balloon wings, Wireworks, 1942

Margaret, top left, Barrow-in-Furness, 1942

*A Watch outside mess hut, Betty French, Peggy Gorham,
Margaret Wilson, 1942*

Margaret marries her Bevin Boy, 1946

*Training for morse slip reader, Margaret Wilson (nee Chapman)
with Margaret Rider, 1944*

Site 30 just before deflation 1942. Rip cord hanging down underneath that triggered explosion if German planes flew into it

Margaret in front of mess tent in Leighton Buzzard

Balloon operators, Margaret, bottom left, 1942

Margaret with Betty French, 1942, the winch for the barrage balloon in the background

THE GOVERNMENT CODE AND CYPHER SCHOOL

Margaret Elizabeth Wilson

*The Government wishes to express
to you its deepest gratitude
for the vital service you performed
during World War II*

David Cameron MP
Prime Minister

May 2010

Gratitude for service certificate

St John, Active Service Edition, front

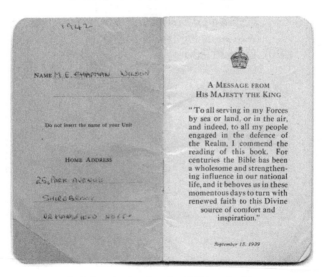

St John, Active Service Edition, inside

RAF service and release book front

RAF release pages

CHAPTER FIVE

RADIOS AT LAST

'The words "I regret to inform you ..."
really brought home the real cost of
what we were doing ...'

– Author

I was lucky enough to be able to fit in a week of home leave before starting my radio operator training. From Barrow I took the train to Chesterfield station, where I was met by my dad. He had caught the train up from Shirebrook with both his and mother's pushbikes, and we rode the nine miles together through the Derbyshire countryside to home.

It was lovely to be home, but I knew it was only for a very short time. I spent nearly all my time with Samuel. In spite of all the letters, or perhaps because of them, we both had plenty to say. This, whilst lovely, was quite unsettling, and I hoped both Samuel and my parents understood. I was also itching to get to my new posting, and it was almost a relief when leave came to an end.

When my week was up I went by train to my new posting, which involved passing through London. I had to change stations and from there on was taken by RAF transport. I knew that London had been bombed, although I saw very little evidence of it where we passed. Later, when we used to come up to London for a weekend off, we would spend the night in the Tube stations. We would sit there all night in a blanket and leave in the morning.

My new posting was to Fighter Command for a month, to RAF West Malling in Kent. The idea was to give me some knowledge of radio operations before I started my actual course. Purely by coincidence my mother had spent time at West Malling when she was in the Land Army in the

Great War. As you can imagine, we had great fun comparing notes when we met again.

This was an operational base, and we could tell that they were very actively involved in the fighting. We had Canadian Spitfire and Mosquito squadrons sortieing out of there. In addition to this we had our own very obvious anti-aircraft guns and searchlights for defence.

A much more discreet part of the activity was the various comings and goings of the Lysander aircraft. They operated mainly at night and would quietly take off with one set of passengers and sometimes returned with others. There were occasions when they did not return at all. Nobody admitted to knowing what they did or where they went, and we all knew better than to ask any questions or talk about it. Years later I realised they were running agents, flying almost at sea level across the channel by night into occupied Europe.

The radio operations were organised into a three-watch system which worked rolling shifts. Basically nights one week, afternoons the next, mornings the next, and so back to nights. This system gave me the opportunity to see how radio operations ran across the full twenty-four hours in the four weeks I was there. They put me on A Watch of the wireless operations group. This was tremendous preparation for when I actually did my wireless operators course as it gave me on-the-job experience so the training would make more sense.

I was lucky as my watch were very generous with their time. As a consequence, I was able to get a taste of most things I was going to have to learn. There were five of us on work experience, and I know the other girls did not have such a good overview with their respective watches.

One of my duties was to act as a messenger, and I was given a bicycle so I could carry important messages from wireless ops to the radar site. This was quite a long way over the other side of the airfield.

I went on duty one night for the 2200-0600hrs shift. When I emerged in the morning, I found that we had suffered a raid during the night: a bomb had dropped right next to the building where we were working, leaving a huge crater which exposed the concrete side of the radio room. When I realised how close it had been I was quite frightened; but on returning for the next shift everything had been restored as if nothing had happened.

They decided that as we were halfway through our fourth week they would move us away from the base. As a result, we were a couple of days early for our course. For once we had time to get settled in before the next round of frantic activity.

The course was at Blackpool, involving an interminable journey almost the entire length of the country. Never mind, at last I was going to start my chosen course. Having had a taste of the radio operator's role, I was even more determined to become one.

The radio operator trainees were lodged together, and we all stayed with Mrs F Robinson in Hornby Road, who looked after us very well – all sixteen of us! She even used to do our laundry. No more crouching over a bucket of water after we had used it for washing! The only thing lacking was enough baths, so we used to go down to the local swimming baths to get clean.

I was in Blackpool for five months, and our lessons were held in the Winter Gardens. When I finished my course I passed the exams quite easily. I had worked really hard, so much so that I was sent to Compton Bassett in Wiltshire, where I was given some more advanced training. I did well enough on that to be invited to consider going for Morse slip reading training [Note 1]. As this was in many ways the pinnacle of radio operating, I enthusiastically agreed.

There was not a course for six months, however, so I was sent to an operational base to get more experience. I was then posted to RAF Syerston near Newark. This was an operational bomber command base, and my first deployment as a qualified wireless operator.

The base radio section operated on the usual three-watch rolling shift system and, again, I was on A Watch, and experienced all aspects of the activities going on.

From that base they flew Wellingtons, Manchesters and Lancasters. These aircraft belonged to 304 and 305 squadrons, which were largely manned by Polish aircrew. You could hear them leaving the base when they were on a raid, and there was then a long, anxious period while we waited for them to come back. A lot of the time, sadly, not all of them returned to us. This generally meant only one thing, although sometimes they had been forced to land at another base.

There were times when some of the losses were so pointless. I remember one day I and another girl, I can't remember her name, witnessed a bomber returning to base after some routine maintenance. It was a Lancaster, and the pilot made a bad approach and clipped the hedge at the edge of the airfield and crashed. There was only the pilot on board, and he was killed when the aircraft exploded in flames.

By the time it had been all sorted out I was near the end of my shift. My shift leader had to get away as his wife was poorly, and he asked me if I would stay on and send the signal. It was the first time I had to send a signal which began with 'I regret to inform you that your son, [...], was killed,' and it really brought home the real cost of what we were doing. It was horrible. Much later, when a memorial was placed there, I found out that he was Canadian. I had thought for years that he was from New Zealand.

We were billeted in huts in a wood. It was lovely, except that we had lots of little visitors. There were mice running everywhere, and I was scared stiff of them, and still am. We also had earwigs and spiders in our beds. The inspired solution to this problem was to give us ear plugs to wear. We felt that our officers had missed the point ...

I loved that job. The hustle and bustle of a busy operational base and the never ending signal traffic made us feel we were part of what was going on. On our days off we used to cycle to all the little villages and walk in the orchards. It was lovely having a taste of what fruit was growing there. On those occasions we could forget the war just for a little while.

Whilst we did not take the terrible risks of the fliers, we were, however, still in the same danger as the ground crew. The only real drawback was the dreadful frequency with which we had to send the 'we regret' signals, and this could get to you if you were not careful. It was something we never really became used to. It was here that the very frequent, if distant, link to Samuel was so welcome. His letters allowed me to escape, if only for a little while, from the painful realities of what we were all doing.

Towards the end of my time there I was offered the chance of promotion to Leading Aircraftwoman. It was very tempting, but the thought of yet another long training course decided me against it. I still, even after all this time, have mixed feelings about that decision.

At the end of six months I was recalled to Compton Bassett. It was time for my Morse slip reader course.

NOTES FOR CHAPTER FIVE

Note 1

Morse Slip Readers

The Morse Slip Readers were highly trained radio operators whose job was not to decode or even transmit messages. Instead they had to listen to enemy wireless traffic and accurately note down the content of each message. Messages were encrypted and would come through in letter groups which had to be accurately recorded and then passed to the decoders. In many ways the MSRs were at the point of the probe that was listening to enemy wireless traffic. This is something which continues to this day.

MSRs generally did not know what the messages said, but that did not matter as they just had to record the dots and dashes accurately. This was done with pencil and paper, not with the benefits of today's audio technology.

It is worth noting that Margaret and her fellow Morse Slip Readers worked eight-hour shifts. It was a job that required incredible focus and concentration. After the war, a series of studies at Cambridge established that twenty minutes was the optimum time that should be spent on a task of this nature without taking a break.

CHAPTER SIX

COME INTO MY PARLOUR ...

---

*'We were taken before a Justice of the
Peace and sworn to secrecy ...'*

– Author

After the busy bomber base at Syerston it felt
quite strange in the quiet world of the radio
school at Compton Bassett, and the Morse Slip
Readers course itself was particularly hard work.
We had to learn how to read Morse code coming
in at the rate of up to sixty words a minute.

Not only did we have to read the signal, we also had to record it accurately on a signal pad with a pencil. We were not allowed to translate the Morse into letters, we just had to record the actual dots and dashes. I think this might have been to prevent us second guessing parts of the signal. Just the raw dots and dashes made us concentrate on the signal and not its possible meaning.

We were also taught other aspects of the use of Morse code. Unfortunately I can say no more about that, as that is one of the things we were sworn to secrecy on. As much as it frustrates historians, including modern-day Bletchley Park, that is the way it has to be.

Sixty words a minute, by any standard, was quite quick, and we were only given two weeks to get to that standard. Because of the requirement to be both accurate and fast, very few of us got through and finished the training.

At the end of the course, those of us who had qualified were taken before a Justice of the Peace. There we were sworn to secrecy. He said to us that we must never talk about what we were doing, that we had to take it to the grave, and he made absolutely sure we understood how very serious this was. We then had to sign the Official Secrets Act before him. We all wondered what we had let ourselves in for.

I was soon to find out. On qualifying as a Morse slip reader and being sworn to secrecy I, with a girl called Margaret Rider was posted to Leighton Buzzard. This was to be my introduction to a very different kind of war.

Leighton Buzzard was a little market town in Bedfordshire with no obvious military connection [Note 1]. It was here that they placed the main communications hub for the country. At one point we had the biggest telephone exchange in the world, but this was only part of what went on there. It was at the centre of a web of stations whose sole job was to listen to the enemy radio traffic.

Leighton Buzzard was known as Q Central, with its outstations, and its location and work was the most closely guarded secret of the war. To begin with it was all a little bit overwhelming, but as with everything else I learned to take things in my stride and tried not to think about it too much.

We were accommodated on the base some way from the communications hub, and there was a mixture of men and women. We would be paraded and then marched over to the communications building ... even there we could not get away from a little bit more marching. Once we arrived at the hub, the men went one way to their work and we girls went to ours.

When we did slip reading we were not allowed to eat with the others. There was a large dining room at the base, but when we came off duty we were told to eat our meals at a separate table well removed from everyone else.

The food was much as you might expect. When we were able to catch breakfast, it was bacon and eggs with baked beans. Sometimes we had a roast dinner, but mainly we had stew. Everywhere I went we seemed to have more stew than anything. As you know, I hated the damned stuff and still do. When we had finished our meal we had to wash our crocks. This entailed going outside, regardless of the weather, to wash our things under a cold water tap.

Those of us who had been posted to Leighton were subjected to more intense training, with constant tests and examinations. One good thing about this was that they told us immediately whether we had passed or not. That was brilliant, as we knew how we were getting on.

Sometimes I was asked to help with the radio operating, and sometimes I worked on the telex machines, a way of sending written messages electronically between stations.

After I had been there for about a month, I was asked to go up to Whitehall for a meeting. I was told to not be too surprised at who I might see or end up talking to. And who did I talk to? Only Winston Churchill! When I arrived there I found out I was being interviewed about a job at the War Cabinet bunker. Mr Churchill was involved in this, and he was very nice and asked me a lot of questions. He said to me, 'Wherever you go to, Margaret, you will be down here. When I come to meetings I will see you.'

At the end of the interview I was shown around and allowed to watch what was going on for a day to see if I felt it was something I wanted to do.

A friend from school was also there, who was later to be killed in the Blitz. In spite of the presence of a friend, I found the interminable steps and the very claustrophobic atmosphere too much for me. It was not only that, the operators were mainly WRNS (Women's Royal Naval Service) and they spent a lot of the time chattering. This was not the way I had been trained and I found it very difficult to concentrate. Apart from that, they were also a bit standoffish and I felt rather isolated. Fortunately, I was allowed to decline the opportunity to work there, and I was sent back to Leighton Buzzard to await another posting.

I had only been back for a couple of days when my new job came through. It was to be at Station X, otherwise known as BP or Bletchley Park.

NOTES FOR CHAPTER SIX

Note 1

Clandestine Operations

A quiet market town with no military presence was chosen as the secret communications centre for Britain as the country prepared for war with Germany in 1937. When hostilities began, 'Q Central' attracted a dozen other clandestine operations set up to defend the country or designed to confuse and undermine enemy morale. The headquarters of radar, RAF Group 60, also came to Leighton Buzzard to be hidden from German attack and to be close to the telephone and radio communications needed to run its vast chain of radar stations. These directed the defending fighters that saved the country in the Battle of Britain and then took the bombing war to Germany.

Close by, for the same reasons of secrecy and safety, were the other crucial operations: the satellite stations of Bletchley Park, the now-famous code-breaking centre; the Met Office at

Dunstable, which gave the all clear for the D-Day landings; Black Ops units that set up false radio stations and wrote propaganda to confuse the enemy; and airfields used for dropping agents behind enemy lines. At Q Central itself was the largest telephone exchange in the world, with more than 1,000 teleprinters communicating with all the armed services in every theatre of war and directing the operations of the secret services.

CHAPTER SEVEN

THE HEART OF THE WEB

---

*'The geese that laid the golden eggs
and never cackled.'*

– Winston Churchill about Bletchley Park

I was ordered to present my kit for inspection and, once it was seen and packed away, I was told that the next day I was to go to Bletchley Park. I was also told that I was to tell no one, and not mention the new posting by name – ever!

The next day Margaret Rider and I and our kit were bundled into a blacked-out RAF transport vehicle and taken to the new posting. On arriving we were put straight onto working a shift without seeing any of the rest of the site. This was to be the pattern for evermore. On finishing this first shift we, with our kit, were then taken to RAF Chicksands [Note 1], again in a blacked-out vehicle. There I was shown my billet and where to get food. Settling in, I had a good night's sleep and was on shift the very next day.

Apart from being on A Watch, the new posting was very different from anything else I had done before. When I entered Bletchley it was like going into another world. Secrecy was everything. If Leighton Buzzard was top secret, Bletchley was ultra.

The only part of Bletchley Park I ever saw was my own work station in my part of my hut. RAF Chicksands was about seventeen miles away, and we were transported to and from work in blacked-out vehicles every time. These were either RAF buses or taxis.

Secrecy was so important that we were not even allowed to know where our place of work was located, and every possible precaution was taken to prevent our finding out. If I had wanted to find it or direct someone, it would have been impossible. This was the great strength of the place. The enemy had no idea it existed, let alone where it was. Even within the world of the armed forces its existence was unknown to all but the very few who needed to know. To the navy it was known as HMS Pembroke V. To the RAF it was known variously as RAF Eastcote, RAF Lime Grove or RAF Church Green. If anybody wanted to write to us, the address was Room 47, Foreign Office.

Before we were allowed anywhere near the place we were briefed about the need for secrecy – again. Security warnings emphasised the importance of discretion even within Bletchley itself:

– do not talk at meals;
– do not talk in the transport;
– do not talk when travelling;
– do not talk in the billet;
– do not talk by your own fireside;
– be careful even in your own hut.

Whilst we were aware in a general sense that 'Careless talk costs lives' and 'Be like Dad, keep Mum, and we had signed the Official Secrets Act, as said this was a whole different level of secrecy. We lived and breathed it our every waking moment. Absolutely no fraternisation was allowed at work. Even when we swapped over at the change of shift, the different shifts were not allowed to see each other. In other words, when we went on shift the previous girls had already left the room. Similarly, we had to leave the room at the end of shift before our reliefs could come in. With one notable exception, the only people I ever met at Bletchley were my shift partner Margaret, and our supervisor.

Margaret and I were billeted together at Chicksands. We ate on our own, never talked to anyone there, and basically lived in our own little bubble. One of my lasting regrets is that Margaret and I lost contact after the war.

Again , I found myself on A Watch. I think there were four watches, and D Watch was used to cover days off, sickness and other absences. There must have been more than two Morse slip readers to a shift, but they would have worked in another hut if there were. In any event, we never met them. Nobody even mentioned the place by name, only referring to it as 'BP'.

I worked there as a Morse slip reader, not as a code breaker as so many people have said. We were the people who provided the decoders with their raw material. Without us listening to the enemy transmissions and accurately jotting down what they were signalling they, the decoders, would have had nothing to work on.

We worked in one particular hut in the grounds of Bletchley, just two of us. We each monitored a small, medium and large radio, and listened to the same thing and jotted it down on paper as it came in. Once we had a few lines of dots and dashes [Note 2] down on the pad, our supervisor would take it into another room. This was usually a sergeant, who would never say anything, and I assume in that other room the dots and dashes we had recorded were rendered into letters. From there I guess it was passed on to the code breakers. I have no idea what happened to it after that.

To be clear, we never knew what the messages were or where they went for sure, and we knew better than to be curious, let alone ask. It was all carefully isolated and we just worked on our little bit.

There was no talking allowed throughout the entire eight-hour shift. If we wanted to go to the toilet we had to put our hand up and the supervisor replaced us.

As far as I can remember, the only time our supervisor spoke to us was when Churchill visited us one night. He told us that we must never mention that Churchill had come to us for as long as we lived. We must take it to the grave.

Churchill came into the hut accompanied by four very big men. He stood behind us and watched what we were doing. After a while he leant towards me and said that he had said he would 'find' me. He either had a brilliant memory, or had been well briefed. Either way, I never saw him again. I did receive a phone call the night he died, though.

Whilst we were on shift there was no break to go to the canteen or anything like that. In all my time there, I never even saw the canteen. We had a cup of tea about halfway through, with a piece of cake – usually fruit cake, full of raisins, sultanas and currants, which I did not like. There was no real break as such as this was brought to us at our workstation. All we ever saw of the place was our station in one part of our particular hut. As said, we never saw a canteen or even the house itself. Too much danger of fraternisation.

We worked on rolling shifts, that is a week on nights, followed by a week of afternoons, and then a week of mornings and so on. This meant that we were never sure what time of day it was. It was like almost permanent jet lag. That on top of the intense and highly focussed work of listening and recording accurately, sometimes up to sixty words a minute, meant that we had little trouble sleeping!

When we came on shift we were never short of a signal, and we could tell our own wireless traffic from the enemy. We and they had had very different training, and you could tell by the way they used the Morse key. Different styles, if you like.

I had arrived in early 1943. Although we never knew who was transmitting, let alone what, there must have been signal traffic from the Italians and Japanese as well as the Germans. We always knew when the Germans' signal ended. They finished their message with the same length of letter groups, which we knew was 'Heil Hitler'.

If the signal did not finish with that length of letter group we guessed that we might have been listening to any of the others, including the Soviets and the Americans. We never knew who, nor did we know, what the signals meant. We just spent all day recording those wretched dots and dashes. You could not make any mistakes, believe me. You had to be very careful.

During that period, my life was mainly lived between my billet at Chicksands and Bletchley Park. We very rarely had time for ourselves. Certainly it was difficult to fit in leave, and I know that I spent two Christmases there. In fact when I was released, they still owed me a lot of leave and sent me some money to make up for it.

We did manage to have a day off occasionally, and used to go into Bedford. I do not think we ever visited the actual town of Bletchley itself, as that was seventeen miles away and Bedford was only seven from our billet. We used to go dancing at the Corn Exchange, and sometimes we would stay over at the YWCA (Young Women's Christian Association). We would stay over unless we were on duty at 0600hrs; in which case we would make sure we were back by 10pm, fresh for the next day. If we did stay overnight, we were back for dinner time so we could be taken for our afternoon shift. We never missed a shift. I shudder to think what would have happened if we had.

It was all a bit of a blur, with one day, week and month rolling into the next. One night I do remember quite clearly was the evening of VE

Day, 8th May 1945. We had been on shift and, as usual, totally isolated from everything. We returned to our billet and, speaking to no one, ate our meal and went to bed. Later on we were woken by drunken singing downstairs. We went down to the common area in our dressing gowns and found people singing and dancing. It was only at that point we learned what had happened. We stayed for some time, joining in the dancing and singing in our night clothes. The next day it was back on shift as if nothing had happened. But we no longer had German signal traffic to listen to. I can only assume that we were listening to either Japanese or Soviet signals. This continued until VJ Day on the 15 August 1945.

We continued our shifts. Secrecy and security was still just as tight. I can only assume we were still monitoring Soviet signal traffic. To be honest, it was such a crazy world it would not have surprised me if it had been American!

I was finally released in 1946 when I decided that I wanted to get married to my Bevin Boy. I left BP for the last time as a WAAF. Mine had been a very interesting war. I had experienced the brutally physical and frankly potentially lethal world of Balloon Command and, apart from a short time at an operational base as a qualified radio operator, my original choice, I had spent most of the war in the murky world of radio intelligence. Today it is called 'elint', electronic intelligence-gathering.

As stated, Churchill referred to the Bletchley staff as 'the geese that laid the golden eggs and never cackled.' That, I think, is something to be quietly proud of.

NOTES FOR CHAPTER SEVEN

Note 1

RAF Chicksands

During the late 1930s the Crown Commission were frantically buying up any properties that might possibly be used for clandestine wartime activity. Curiously, Bletchley was not one of them. That had to be bought privately. Chicksands was one of those purchased in 1937. It was named after Chicksands Priory, the 12th Century Gilbertine Monastery whose ruins were located within the grounds.

Initially the place was requisitioned by the Royal Navy, but after nine months was taken over by the RAF. A sigint, or signals intelligence, station was established. They spent the war listening to enemy signals and passing them on to the decoding station at Bletchley.

The site was allocated to the Americans in 1950, with the RAF acting as hosts. The Americans withdrew in 1996, and the RAF connection ended when it was taken over by the Army Intelligence Corps in 1997.

Note 2

Dots and Dashes

Trying to get any idea about what Margaret did as a Morse slip reader was impossible. All she would say was:

'It was all in Morse code, but Morse code is definitely not just dots and dashes. There were different ways of putting things down, and then you had to work out what that one meant … it might mean a dot and a dash. You had to work it out. I am not telling you anymore. We were told to take it to the grave. None of the other girls have talked, so that is where it is going.'

Make of that what you will.

REFLECTIONS

Finally, after three years of an almost monastic existence, I took my release in the April of 1946. It was time to go home and marry Samuel, who had been such a stalwart support throughout the whole nonsense. Samuel never had any idea of what I was doing or where I was during the entire war. Bless him, I was unable to make him much the wiser afterwards.

Shortly after leaving I received a letter from the Air Ministry, which contained a cheque for fifty-three days' pay as compensation for the leave I had been unable to take whilst at Bletchley.

I then received a second letter informing me that if there was an emergency I could be recalled at twenty-four hours' notice. They added that if I had married and had children they could come with me. The children would be 'well looked after and properly educated'.

I showed the letter to my new employer and they were perfectly understanding.

It seemed I was to be in the outer reaches of the web of Bletchley for at least the next seven years, the time period a member of the armed forces remained in 'active reserve'. I was, however, never called upon, and my life moved on.

A NOTE FROM THE FAMILY

Margaret (Nanna) continued in the WAAF for a short time after the end of WW2, and was officially demobbed on 19 April 1946. Her exit from the armed forces came after her wedding to her much-loved husband Sam on the 2 February 1946, and she settled into married life, welcoming their first child, Brian, on the 18 December 1946.

Margaret has always enjoyed meeting new people, and through her employment and charitable endeavours she worked to support the local community. One of her first post-war roles was supporting the clerk to the parish council, and she also became a governor for Brian's school, continuing to do so when her daughter Kay was born.

A variety of retail roles followed and included Weber's Grocers in Mansfield, Brimbles Butchers, a fish & chip shop in Warsop, and a long-standing role serving in the café, working with a variety of family members and forging a multitude of enduring friendships. She also became an active member of the local Brownies and Guides, earning the title of Tawny Owl.

Margaret joined the British Legion in 1946 and continued to support their work as a poppy seller, collecting funds and organising others to help. This resulted in her becoming a Poppy Day organiser and being given the responsibility of becoming a Poppy Day parade organiser. Margaret also helped establish the Royal British Legion women's branch, Shirebrook, and acted as its chairman for many years. This included the honour of being the standard-bearer on many occasions.

Her son, Brian, recalls one of his earliest memories, of his mother, the parade organiser, the local policeman, and a variety of volunteers being in the front room counting the proceeds of the poppy collection. So successful was the collection that the next day the ever-supportive Sam, a keen gardener, then transported it down to TSB on Main Street in his wheelbarrow!

Margaret and Sam loved going on holiday together and took many trips, including Ibiza, Tunisia, and taking the grandchildren to see

Mickey Mouse at Disneyland Paris. She really wanted to meet Mickey! One of their favourite places was the caravan and beach chalet that they purchased at Mablethorpe and Sutton-on-Sea, where Sam and Margaret could be found looking after their grandchildren and feeding any additional friends that had been made that day. Margaret's ability to cook a roast dinner for at least seven in the beach hut should not be underestimated! Margaret and Sam became part of the seaside community and considered it a second home, with many friends made. Never far from wanting to support her charities, Margaret was even asked to act as standard-bearer for the Mablethorpe Parade, which she of course relished.

Margaret was also an active member of the WRVS (Women's Royal Voluntary Service), and ran a variety of self-help groups helping older members of the community to come together to have afternoon tea, play Dominos and Bingo, and enjoy the occasional tea dance. She also helped with Meals on Wheels and visiting those members who were ill at home or in hospital, with Sam supporting her by acting as taxi driver for both Margaret and the members. Unfortunately, this activity had to come to an end when she reached seventy-five as she could not gain insurance to run the group. This did not stop her raising money for the local church and selling raffle tickets for the charities she wanted to support.

Following the death of Sam, Margaret's sight began to deteriorate, and she joined Derbyshire Sight Support. It was at a session organised by this group that she was introduced to Blind Veterans, who have supported her in understanding more about her condition and helped her establish a new routine after his death. This has included residential stays at Blind Veterans facilities in Wales and Brighton, which Margaret enjoys as there are a whole new set of people to get to know! A particular highlight for Margaret was attending a "Lest we Forget" garden party at Buckingham Palace, as she does like to meet a Royal. Blind Veterans also organised that Margaret attend the Remembrance Day parade in London, acting as wreath layer on behalf of the organisation, a role that those of us watching at home enjoy as she is very easy to spot!

Margaret was awarded a medal in recognition of her service at Bletchley Park. She has attended a variety of events there, and they always ask if she is up to speaking to other visitors, announcing that she is on site and encouraging people to ask her any questions. As you will now know from reading this book, she will only tell you so much ...

Margaret continues with her charity work, going into her great-grandchildren's schools to give talks about her experiences in WW2, taking her gas mask, ration book and WAAF medals with her.

She also spends a huge amount of time talking remotely to groups within Blind Veterans and other groups of veterans.

There are most likely other things that have been missed out here, as Margaret has done such a lot in her 100 years and for so many people. As a family we are very proud of her and what she has achieved.

Thank you to Simon and the wider team for compiling her memories into this book. It will serve as a great testament to show the great-grandchildren, and all who follow, what she has achieved.

Thank you, all.

ADDITIONAL INFORMATION

BLETCHLEY PARK

The activities at Bletchley Park during the war, and later, were up there amongst the most closely guarded secrets of the war. Not only its activities but also its location was hush-hush. As indicated by Margaret, many of the people working at Bletchley had very little, if any, idea of where it was or what was going on. Every precaution was taken to ensure that the separate parts of activities there remained so.

And yet it very nearly didn't happen. In the late 1930s, when the Crown Commission were frantically buying up any property which might serve for clandestine activity, when it came to Bletchley there was no budget. Admiral Sinclair, head of the Secret Intelligence Service, also known as MI6, bought the house and fifty-eight acres of ground privately for just under half a million pounds in today's money.

In most ways it was ideal. It was close to the main West Coast rail route and Watling Street, the modern A5. It was also easily accessible from both Oxfordshire and Cambridge, from whose universities they hoped to recruit code breakers. Unfortunately, one of them, who joined in 1943 from Cambridge, was a Soviet mole.

With the Post Office repeater station at nearby Fenny Stratford and the powerful radio station at Rugby, only thirty miles away, the telecommunications and radio links were first class.

With the establishment of Leighton Buzzard as the national communications hub, and RAF Chicksands as sigint collecting centre, Bletchley was truly at the heart of a web of intelligence gathering from the ether. As part of the security measures, Leighton was known as Q Central, Bletchley as Station X, and Chicksands as Station Y. Other security methods to conceal both the function and location of this web have already been mentioned in Margaret's story.

The Central Cypher and Decoding Centre at Bletchley was tasked to eavesdrop on enemy radio traffic. The German traffic proved indecipherable, however, due to a machine called Enigma, which was the ultimate device for scrambling messages. Until a working model was ripped out of the sinking U110 by a young Royal Naval sub-lieutenant they were having a pretty hard time of it. (In spite of Hollywood's story to the contrary, it was the British and not the Americans who did this.)

The Germans never learned we had the Enigma machine. It was vitally important that they never did, and this involved some dreadful dilemmas: if an enemy knew that we knew their codes they would have changed them and we would have been back in the dark again; sometimes the information gained could not be used for fear of giving the game away; Churchill had to let the bombing of Coventry happen, because if he had ordered special precautions the enemy would have known we had Enigma.

Similarly, naval Intelligence had long since cracked the Japanese naval codes. They were fully aware the British raid on the Italian naval base at Taranto had excited Japanese interest. They followed the preparations for Pearl Harbour almost from its inception. If they had told the Americans it risked their knowledge of the Japanese codes getting out. There was also the minor matter of Churchill being frantic for the Americans to become involved.

At its height Bletchley had over 10,000 people working there from all three services, plus civilians. It is estimated that seventy-five percent of them were women. It continued throughout the war, and beyond, as a vital intelligence gathering centre.

In 1946 it changed its name to RAF Eastcote. In the 1950s the operation was transferred to Cheltenham. It is now simply referred to as GCHQ. Whilst its location is now known, its activities remain just as vital and just as shrouded in security.

WOMEN'S AUXILIARY AIR FORCE

In the Great War women served In in the Women's Royal Air Force during the years 1918 to 1920, after which it was disbanded. Women were not given the opportunity to serve until the formation of the RAF Auxiliary Territorial Service companies, which were formed in 1938. In June 1939, the existing forty-eight companies were amalgamated into the Women's Auxiliary Air Force. The individual members of this force were known as WAAFs.

Conscription for women did not start until 1941, and then only for those between twenty and thirty years of age. They were given the choice of the auxiliary services or the factories.

Women recruited into the WAAF were given basic training at one of five sites, though not all of the sites ran training simultaneously. The five sites were at West Drayton, Harrogate, Bridgnorth, Innsworth and Wilmslow. From 1943, all WAAF basic training was conducted at Wilmslow.

Women were not allowed to act as air crew or adopt any combat role. However, in 1944 WAAF nursing orderlies elected to be deployed into the flying ambulances. These ambulances transported casualties from the fighting in Europe to England through still hostile skies. Having said that, the WAAFs stood the same risks of injury whilst serving on the numerous operational bases by enemy action as their male colleagues.

WAAFs were actively deployed in a whole range of activities from providing crews for barrage balloons, packing parachutes, radar, radio, telex and telecommunications, iconically working the plot, and accurately depicting the positions of both friendly and enemy aircraft. This was particularly critical during the battles over Kent in 1940. They also carried out catering, clerical and transport roles. They were involved in meteorological work, cyphers and Morse slip reading. Code breaking also fell within their range of activities. Gradually they became an important part of the war effort.

At one stage the WAAF were attracting 2,000 recruits a month, and within a very short time they had established themselves as a vital part of the RAF strength. This was particularly so at the clandestine world of Bletchley Park, where women made up seventy-five percent of the 10,000 personnel involved in its work. This, however, did not prevent them being paid only two-thirds of that paid to their male counterparts.

After the war the strength of the WAAF was steadily reduced through the process of demobilisation to only a few hundred. In 1949, it was renamed the Women's Royal Air Force. Finally, in 1994, the female and male parts were came under the Royal Air Force, with all roles open to women, including female fighter pilots.

MORSE CODE

Invented by Samuel Morse in the 1840s for the new electric telegraph. Short electronic pulse to signify a dot, a long pulse to signify a dash. Can also be used with a signal lamp, particularly at sea and air to ground.

		Numbers
a ·-	n -·	0 -----
b -····	o ---	1 ·----
c -·-·	p ·--·	2 ··---
d -··	q --·-	3 ···--
e ·	r ·-·	4 ····-
f ··-·	s ···	5 ·····
g --·	t -	6 -····
h ····	u ··-	7 --···
i ··	v ···-	8 ---··
j ·---	w ·--	9 ----·
k -·-	x -··-	0 -----
l ·-··	y -·--	
m --	z --··	

GLOSSARY OF TERMS

Some terms or words with which people may be unfamiliar.

Agent
Person who is secretly inserted into enemy territory to gather information and enable the destruction of their personnel and property if required.

Aircrew
Air Force crew who actually fly. Pilots, navigators, air gunners and so on.

Anti-aircraft gun
Weapon designed to shoot either solid or exploding projectiles at enemy aircraft in order to destroy or force to the ground.

Basic training

A period of short, sharp training designed to turn civilians into service personnel as quickly as possible.

Beasting

The process of chivvying, harrying and putting recruits. Designed to develop tolerance of nonsense and resilience under pressure. The politically correct and champions of mediocrity would call it bullying. It is important to remember that Michelangelo's 'David' was not carved with a butter knife.

Bed pack

The end product of the process of stripping your bedclothes off the bed and making a perfectly symmetrical and wrinkle-free pile. Easier said than done.

Blacked-out vehicle

A vehicle with the windows covered in such a way that only the driver can see out.

Blackout

The process of making sure that no light inside a building can be seen outside to prevent lights acting as a guide to enemy bombers.

Blitz

From the German 'Blitzkreig' or 'lightening war'. In this case it refers to the attempted destruction of London from the air.

Bombs

A canister or casing containing either explosives or flammable material. Designed to blow apart or burn personnel and property.

'Careless talk costs lives' or 'Be like Dad, keep Mum'

Two very common messages on posters to remind people to keep their mouths shut about their work or anything else.

Code breaker

Person employed to discover the real meaning of secret and scrambled messages.

Conscription
The unavoidable requirement for men, and later women, of fighting age to join one of the services and later the coal mines. There were a few reserved occupations but not many. Most people had no choice but to fight, but they could choose which service.

Convoys
The German submarine fleet was nearly all at sea when war broke out. Britain had to import food, fuel and equipment and it had to come by sea. Merchant ships were organised into groups protected by warships to carry these goods. This was the convoy system.

Demob
At the end of the war those who had been conscripted were released back to their civilian lives. This was known as 'demobilisation' or 'demob'.

Detonator
A small amount of explosive which explodes the main charge in a bomb or artillery shell.

Dig for victory
We could not feed ourselves and many food carrying ships were sunk. Every patch of available ground was turned into growing vegetables. Known as 'dig for victory'.

Elint
Electronic intelligence gathering.

Enigma
A very clever German encoding machine. Could change the code with every key stroke. Impossible to break until one was captured. The knowledge of that capture was top secret.

Gas mask
Every man, woman and child was required to carry one of these at all times. Basically a hood with airproof goggles built in, with a charcoal filter over the mouth and nose to remove any poisonous gas.

Greatcoat
Every service person was issued with an extremely heavy winter coat. It was full length and known as a 'Malmesbury warm' or 'great coat'.

Ground crew
Air Force personnel not involved in flying. In other words, the people supporting the flyers, feeding, maintaining aircraft, defending the base, communications, logistics and so on.

Hydrogen
Highly flammable gas used to inflate barrage balloons.

Lancaster
Very successful heavy bomber used by the RAF. Powered by four Merlin engines and carried a crew of six or seven.

Lysander
A high-wing mono plane, very slow and steady, used to infiltrate agents and equipment into occupied Europe at night.

Mosquito
Very fast fighter bomber made of balsa wood and powered by two Merlin engines. Almost invisible to radar – first stealth aircraft? – and carried a crew of two. When deployed to the Far East known as the 'termite's delight'.

NCO
Non-commissioned officer.

Officer
Person in the armed forces who holds the Sovereign's commission to be in charge of other personnel below their own rank.

Operational base
An area from which aircraft were deployed to actively seek out and destroy enemy personnel, equipment, property and infrastructure.

Peeping Tom
From the legend of Lady Godiva of Coventry. A person who hides themselves so they can observe naked females without being discovered.

Polish aircrew
After the fall of Poland many of the Poles fought in the Battle for France and then in the RAF. Nearly 150 were involved in the Battle of Britain and many more flew with the RAF during the war.

Lashing
Line or rope to secure one object to another.

Manchester
Under-powered bomber a bit like a two-engined Lancaster. Phased out fairly quickly.

MI6
Part of the secret intelligence service. Military Intelligence, Department 6. Tasked with causing rather than discovering disruption.

Morse slip reader
Highly trained radio operator who listened to and recorded enemy signals with pencil and paper. This was then sent to the code breakers.

Potato cake
A filling and popular cake made of potatoes, which were unrationed. Made of potato, plain flour, egg, onion, salt and pepper.

Rationing
Allocation of food. Combat troops in the field had 'compo' rations. Compo dating from the war was still being used in the 1960s.

Red cap
Slang for a military policeman.

Release
Regular servicemen were released from their contract, not demobilized.

Shrapnel
Pieces of the metal casing of a bomb or shell which fly about when the bomb or shell explodes. Invented by Colonel Shrapnel. First used by the British in 1804.

Sigint Collection Centre
A centre for collecting signals intelligence/ listening to enemy radio traffic.

Signal traffic
A collective term for wireless messages.

SIS
Secret Intelligence Service. Tasked with preventing the gathering of information or causing of damage to people, property and infrastructure at home and causing the same abroad.

Snow drop
Slang for RAF policeman.

Sortieing
The action of an aircraft taking off to seek and carry out actions harmful to the enemy.

Spitfire
Single-engine fighter aircraft. In the minority at the Battle of Britain but grabbed all the glory. Over 22,000 made and nearly seventy still flying.

Square-bashing
Learning how to march, both individually and as part of a formation.

Streaker
A person who runs about naked in public in order to shock.

The General Strike
A nine-day strike of all coal miners. The owners of coal mines had halved the wages and wanted to make them lower with longer hours. Miners were supported by transport and heavy industry workers also striking. Only nine days in May 1926, but had great impact

The Great Depression
The economic downturn that lasted from 1929 to 1939. The worst economic slump in modern history.

Tin lid
Slang for steel helmet. Modern version is the 'battle bowler'.

VE Day
The day World War II finished in Europe with the unconditional surrender of Germany.

VJ Day
The end of the war with victory over Japan.

War Cabinet bunker
Very deep bomb shelters where the War Cabinet could meet in safety.

Watch
Service term for a shift.

Wellington
Very effective medium bomber designed by Barnes Wallis. Revolutionary geodesic design.

Printed in Great Britain
by Amazon

24659761R00081